Dragonflies

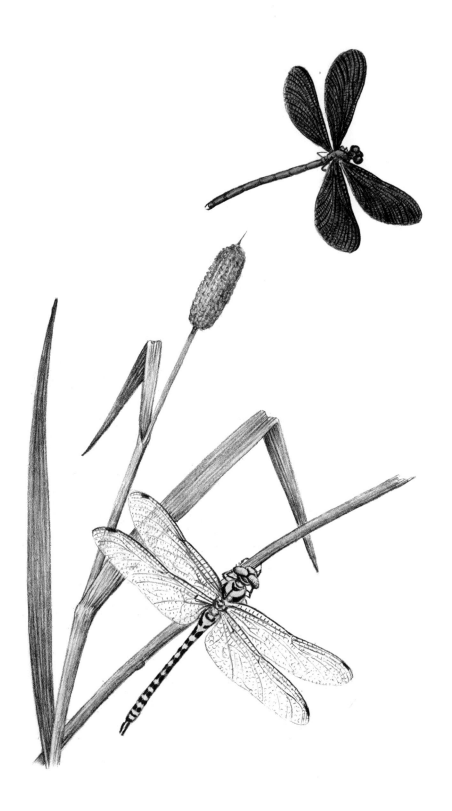

Hilda Simon

Dragonflies

Illustrated by the author

THE VIKING PRESS   NEW YORK

First Edition

Copyright © 1972 by Hilda Simon
All rights reserved
First published in 1972 by The Viking Press, Inc.
625 Madison Avenue, New York, N.Y. 10022
Published simultaneously in Canada by
The Macmillan Company of Canada Limited
Library of Congress catalog card number: 71–185347
SBN 670–28147–6
595.7 Insects
Printed in U.S.A.
1   2   3   4   5   76   75   74   73   72

In memoriam
Dr. Julius Grober
Professor of Tropical Medicine at the University of Jena,
a medical explorer and nature enthusiast

Contents

List of Illustrations

List of Illustrations

List of Illustrations

Today I saw the dragon-fly
Come from the wells where he did lie.
An inner impulse rent the veil
Of his old husk: from head to tail
Came out clear plates of sapphire mail.
He dried his wings: like gauze they grew;
Thro' crofts and pastures wet with dew
A living flash of light he flew.

Alfred, Lord Tennyson.

Miracle at Dawn

In the gray light at the break of dawn, the swirling mists over the pond seem to have a life of their own as they lift and drift downward and lift again, revealing tall bulrushes that stand like sentries in the milky fog. The pond lies in the absolute silence of the pre-dawn period. At this time, no twittering of a bird is heard, no frog gives voice to a throaty croak. This is the in-between hour when the creatures of the night have ended their hunt and have retired to sleep, while those active by day are not yet quite ready to stir.

Suddenly something moves on one of the bulrushes. A brownish, peculiar-looking creature that resembles an overgrown earwig has firmly gripped the bulrush stem onto which it had crawled out of the water below during the night. For several hours it had remained there motionless, but now the resting period is over. Its skin splits across the

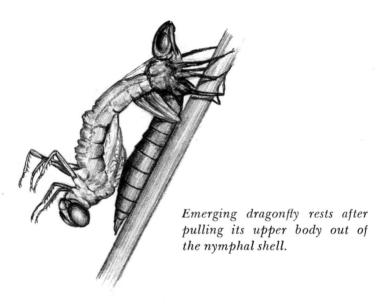

Emerging dragonfly rests after pulling its upper body out of the nymphal shell.

head and down the back, and through the split is thrust a head belonging to a different type of creature. This new being pushes upward and forward, withdrawing its legs and the entire front part of its body from the old skin, which retains its original shape and position, still gripping the bulrush stem.

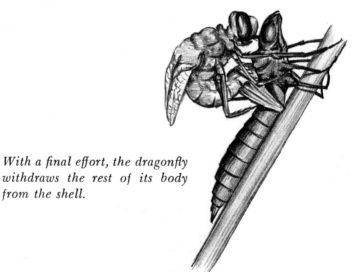

With a final effort, the dragonfly withdraws the rest of its body from the shell.

After resting for a little while, the newly emerging creature makes a final effort and pulls the rest of its body out of the sheath of its former self, disclosing crumpled wings and a misshapen form. It is hard to believe that soon this bedraggled thing will be a beautiful, glittering dragonfly soaring through the air on translucent wings, capable of traveling thirty miles an hour.

Still grasping its old shell, the adult dragonfly again rests, as though exhausted by its efforts. With every passing minute, its appearance changes: The wings stretch and expand, displaying an intricate network of veins, as the body hardens and begins to show its colors and patterns.

Several hours have passed. The sun is long since bright in the sky, and the dragonfly, its wings fully outstretched, is ready for the maiden flight which will take it into the world of sun and air, far away from the murky depths of the pond where it spent the first part of its life.

Survivors of a Distant Past

Accustomed as we are to our natural environment, it is difficult for us to visualize a world in which plant and animal life was so totally different as to have hardly any resemblance to that of the present. Some 200,000,000 years ago, in the carboniferous period, trees and flowers did not exist. There were no mammals, no birds, and none of the flying insects—no bees, butterflies, or beetles—that live in a close relationship with blossoming plants of all kinds, from grasses and grains to bushes and shrubs. Only amphibians and many diverse kinds of reptiles, as well as some insects, were found on dry land. While these ancient insects had the basic, distinctive characteristics of their group—a body divided into three main parts, head, thorax, and abdomen; six legs; antennae; and wings—they are called "primitive" insects by biologists because they lacked the more complex, advanced features which distinguish the highly developed insects that appeared in later ages.

The oldest-known winged insect, Stilbocrocis heeri, *from the Upper Carboniferous period, once considered to be the ancestor of all winged insects—an assumption recently challenged by some scientists.*

The oldest kind of insect still living today is the all-too-well-known cockroach. The modern cockroach differs very little from its ancestor of some 250,000,000 years ago. While this fact will hardly help to make the average housewife feel more kindly inclined toward what she considers to be an obnoxious household pest, it does make this insect interesting as a kind of "living fossil." It may be added that cockroaches have many other fascinating features, including a learning ability that surpasses that of most other insects. They are among the very few of their group, for instance, that can be taught to find their way through a maze. They can master this problem because they are capable of remembering the errors that lead them into the dead-end entrances and of avoiding them next time around. Roaches are prime examples of the fact that being a so-called primitive form does not preclude any animal from being highly successful in the struggle for survival.

Dragonflies are also very ancient insects, even though their ancestry does not reach quite as far back as that of the roaches. All the same, we know that giant dragonflies flew and hunted their prey before the Age of the Dinosaurs—long before the first lizard-like ancestor of the birds appeared on the scene. Fossil impressions indicate that these ancient dragonflies had a wingspread of up to thirty inches, making them the largest insects that ever lived.

Except for their large size, these dragonflies of long ago resembled in all their basic body structures our modern dragonflies, and we assume, although we cannot know for certain, that their way of life and development were also similar. The fossil record in this case, as in most others, is not complete. No fossil impression of a dragonfly larva, the insect's immature form, has ever been found; and even if it were, many questions would remain.

Among the unanswered questions is whether the larvae of the giants of the past lived in the water as do those of

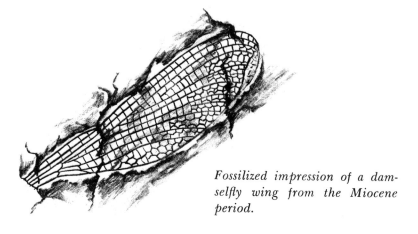

Fossilized impression of a damselfly wing from the Miocene period.

their modern descendants. If so—and biologists are inclined to believe they did—these almost foot-long monsters must have been fierce hunters and killers, for even a modern two-inch dragonfly larva is a formidable predator for its size, and one of the most rapacious of all insects.

Throughout the Age of the Dinosaurs, dragonflies were considerably smaller than their giant ancestors, but otherwise unchanged—a fact attested to by some remarkably well-preserved fossils from that period. Dragonflies have remained basically the same, except for size, throughout the tens of millions of years during which countless, once-common plant and animal forms were replaced by other, different organisms—including man, that latecomer on the world's stage. By the time man appeared, the plains and forests of our planet bore little resemblance to the landscape in which the dragonfly ancestors flew and hunted. By surviving unchanged throughout the continuous changes in the environment (including its recent deterioration from man-made pollution), by actually holding their own in this altered world, dragonflies have created their own impressive success story.

In keeping with their ancient ancestry, dragonflies have no close relatives among insects and are placed in an order all by themselves. In biological classification, the order ranks below the class, which is a comprehensive group of animals—or plants—having certain common characteristics. Thus, mammals are a class, and so are birds, and fish, and, of course, insects. The order is a group of more closely related animals within the larger class grouping, differing widely in the number of successively smaller subdivisions known as the

Damselfly (left) and dragonfly in typical resting positions. Their habit of resting with wings outspread helps distinguish the true dragonflies from damselflies in the field.

family, genus, and species. One of the smallest insect orders contains only one family with a single genus comprising nineteen species. At the other end of the scale, the order of the beetles has dozens of families, with hundreds of genera and some 250,000 species.

Dragonflies are well between these two extremes. Modern classification has grouped these insects in two suborders that together make up the order of Odonata. In one of these suborders are the slender members called damselflies, which are easily distinguished at a glance by their habit of holding the wings closed above the body when resting. Their usually more robust cousins, which always sit with wings stretched out flat, are known as the true dragonflies. This distinction does not apply in other languages: in French, all members of the Odonata are called *demoiselles,* and in German, *Libellen,* which is the old scientific name for the entire group.

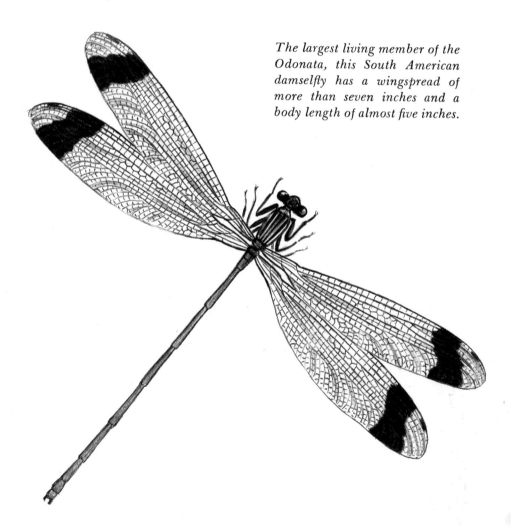

The largest living member of the Odonata, this South American damselfly has a wingspread of more than seven inches and a body length of almost five inches.

Although it does not attain the measurements of its South American cousin, the heavier body and larger head and thorax of this African dragonfly, shown here in natural size, makes it appear bigger than the exceedingly slender giant damselfly.

Damselflies are divided into twelve families, dragonflies into only six. Altogether, there are about 4500 species, found throughout the world wherever the insects have access to the fresh water that all of them need for the development of their young, except for one interesting Hawaiian species, which is wholly terrestrial.

Dragonflies are among our largest insects. Although no modern species comes even close in size to the giants of the

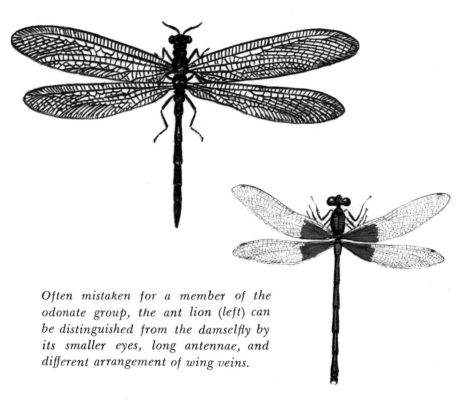

Often mistaken for a member of the odonate group, the ant lion (left) can be distinguished from the damselfly by its smaller eyes, long antennae, and different arrangement of wing veins.

past, the largest living odonate, a native of the South American tropics, measures seven and one-half inches across the outspread wings and has a body length of approximately five inches. The wingspread in dragonflies averages from three to four inches, and in damselflies less than that.

Most members of the group are brightly colored in beautiful hues and patterns. In the majority of species, these colors are concentrated on the slender body, while the intricately veined wings are more or less transparent and colorless. However, quite a number of species have either colored spots on their wings or colored veins crisscrossing a colorless wing membrane. Among damselflies, several species are distinguished by solid-colored wings often gleaming in dark steel blues and greens. Certain tropical dragonflies have multicolored wings that look like miniature stained-glass windows.

Colors among dragonflies may be the result either of pigments or of physical structure. All the beautiful metallic or iridescent blues and greens and some bright reds, as well as the brilliant multicolored hues of the dragonflies' eyes, are exclusively structural. Structural colors are created by the refraction of light as it strikes submicroscopic tissue structures. By reflecting some and absorbing all the other component colors of white light, very pure, gleaming colors are produced. Pigment colors, on the other hand, need a chemical substance to reflect selectively certain light waves, and the hues thus produced are neither as pure nor as brilliant as the structural colors.

Dragonflies are predominantly creatures of the air and the sun. During the daylight hours, they are almost constantly on the wing as they hunt the insects that are their exclusive food. Many are great travelers—one species is aptly called the "globetrotter"—often covering long distances in

Libellula depressa, *a common European species, and its close relative* Libellula quadrimaculata *have been known to make long-distance migrations. In 1862, an estimated throng of two thousand million was observed flying by at a height of thirty feet, in Germany's East Prussian province, from early morning until late in the afternoon.*

A dragonfly zeroing in on a mosquito. Despite their more advanced flight apparatus, flies, gnats, and mosquitoes are unable to outmaneuver the agile "dragons."

the search for insect prey, which they always catch in flight. Certain species of dragonflies migrate in a manner similar to that of the famed monarch butterfly, congregating in large numbers and traveling great distances during these flights.

Because the prey of the adults consists largely of flies, gnats, and mosquitoes, dragonflies are beneficial insects. Their nickname, "mosquito hawk," is well earned. They have been observed hovering above cattle, very much in the manner of certain birds, and darting among the big mammals to capture the bot flies and stable flies that always accompany, and so often torture and injure, these herd animals while they graze. The dragonflies' keen vision, agility, and strength enable them to catch even large and fast-flying members of the insect clan. Only occasionally can dragonflies be considered anything but beneficial—when they prey upon honeybees, for example, and this habit, ascribed especially to one species, is encountered infrequently.

During their larval development, nearly all members of the Odonata live in the water. The larvae do not resemble the adults at all, and for many centuries the relationship between the immature and mature stages of these insects was unrecognized. In the seventeenth century, dragonfly larvae were described as water "lizards" that prey upon fish. Actually, the old name *libellae* for dragonflies was given originally to the immature forms by a sixteenth-century naturalist who thought that the head of a damselfly larva resembled a hammer head. Later, after the aquatic larva and the flying adult had been found to be different forms of the same insect, the name was applied to dragonflies in general.

In most cases, dragonfly and damselfly larvae inhabit such bodies of water as ponds, lakes, streams, and brooks. But some species deposit their eggs in temporary pools, and their larvae develop most rapidly, completing their larval stage in a few weeks, while most others take more than a year, some remaining as larvae for as long as five years. One of the strangest breeding locations is used by a tropical South American species, whose females lay their eggs in the water accumulated at the base of huge leaves of the so-called air plants that grow on the branches and trunks of large trees in the tropical rain forests. In these tiny pools high above the ground, the larvae feed on other aquatic insects sharing this unique water supply, and thus are able to complete their development.

The Hawaiian species mentioned earlier as a wholly terrestrial one is a reminder that in nature, with its infinitely varied ways, there is hardly a rule that does not have its exception. Actually, the family of damselflies to which this species belongs has other members whose larvae leave the water to hunt for insects in wet and muddy locations. But the Hawaiian species is the only one that is unable to swim and has no mechanism for breathing in the water—the only member of the entire order that differs from all the rest in this respect. All other dragonfly and damselfly larvae, even though they vary considerably in color, shape, size, and choice of aquatic habitat, are equipped with gills that permit them to breathe underwater. The gills may be either internal or visible as taillike appendages at the tip of the abdomen. The latter arrangement is found in damselfly larvae and is one of the major points of distinction between damselflies and dragonflies.

It was inevitable that so large, beautiful, and unusual an insect as the dragonfly should have fascinated people throughout the ages. This fascination took many different forms, ranging from fearful superstitions, expressed by such names as "snake doctors" and "stingers," to the reverence with which some South American Indians regard local dragonflies, believed to be the spirits of departed human beings.

Poets and artists of many countries have immortalized dragonflies in their songs and works of art. Especially in the Orient, home of some of the most striking species, painters and sculptors have for centuries vied with each other in artistic representations of these insects. Dragonflies have been cast in silver and gold, with inset eyes of precious stones, and they appear in paintings with delicate colors on silk and parchment. In Japan, dragonflies have historically occupied an important place in both art and literature as the symbol of victory in battle. It is perhaps not surprising that one of the leading centers of modern biological research on dragonflies is located in that country.

Decorative and beneficial, dragonflies are worthwhile subjects for study by expert and amateur alike. In the pages that follow, we shall take a closer look at the individual dragonfly, its habits, its anatomical structures, and the special features which enable this insect to hold its own in an often drastically changed environment.

Life in the Sun

From the moment the newly emerged dragonfly takes to the air until the end of its life several months later, it will stay on the wing the greater part of the day, hunting and capturing its prey in flight. Most dragonflies are creatures of the sunlight, and often seem to disappear completely when the skies become cloudy and overcast. During periods of cloudy and rainy weather, these sun-loving species can occasionally be found resting, in an almost trancelike condition, in a hiding place well protected by vegetation or overhanging rocks.

There are, however, quite a number of species that fly and hunt whether or not the sun is shining, and even a few that seem to welcome the absence of the sun, some of which hunt in the twilight very much like bats and swifts. The strange South American species that include the largest known member of the Odonata fly ghostlike on almost invisible wings at dusk in the tropical forests. Little wonder that the Indians believed these insects to be the spirits of recently deceased persons.

A green darner with a captured mosquito.

The typical dragonfly, such as the common green darner, known popularly as the darning needle, is on the wing almost constantly during sunny days, swooping down to capture flies, wasps, mosquitoes, beetles, and other flying insects. It fears neither poison stings nor sharp mandibles, and is a match for practically any insect it encounters. Dragonflies have voracious appetites, and will stuff themselves with food as fast as they can catch their prey. After a meal, they usually clean their faces, and especially their eyes, with their spiny legs. This cleaning process is very thorough and may take quite some time.

Damselflies are relatively weak fliers and often have a fluttering, rather slow flight that makes them fairly easy to catch. Most dragonflies are noted for their strong, swift flight and their great agility. Some soar high into the sky and travel great distances. The average speed of the larger species is about thirty miles per hour, although a speed as high as sixty miles an hour for short distances has been reported. Individuals of one cosmopolitan species were collected two hundred miles from shore as they alighted on ships. Undoubtedly, of course, these adventurous travelers were aided by tail winds during their long-distance flight.

The agility of the larger dragonflies is proverbial among naturalists, their swift, darting flight being hard even for the eye to follow. They are among the most frustrating insects from a collector's point of view, for they seem to be able to read his mind and outwit him at every turn. A dragonfly patrolling a pond from a nearby rock, swooping down to capture mosquitoes or to scoop up a mouthful of midges, and then returning to its perch on the rock after each venture, may seem an ideal target for a collector. There it is, clinging to the exact spot on the rock it has been returning to for the past half hour. Hopefully, the collector takes up his position, standing motionless not far from the rock, waiting for his prospective victim to return. There it comes!—and flits right past him to perch on another rock well out of his reach! This game can be repeated any number of times, and usually ends with a tired, maddened, frustrated collector who has nothing to show for his pains except a number of mosquito bites, and a nonchalant dragonfly which, if we were talking of a human being, would certainly be described as "laughing up his sleeve."

It seems clear that dragonflies need special equipment for their unique way of life, and they do in fact have a number of body features not found in any other insect. One of the most striking of these is the head with its enormous eyes. Though less pronounced in the damselflies, the huge, bulging eyes of most dragonflies tend to overspread the top

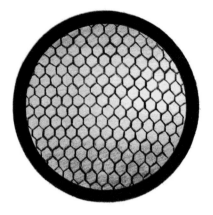

Small section of a dragonfly's eye, greatly magnified. These colors are structural hues, caused by light reflection.

of the head and meet in what is called an "eye seam." As in all adult insects, these are compound eyes, made up of many individual organs of sight. These individual units, called ommatidia, appear on the surface as neat, little six-sided facets joined in honeycomb fashion. Actually, these facets are a protective covering corresponding to the cornea in the human eye, and consist of chitin—the same substance that forms all insects' outer-body covering. Beneath each facet we find a tiny crystal-clear cone ending in a retinal rod that leads into the optic nerve. Each ommatidium is sur-

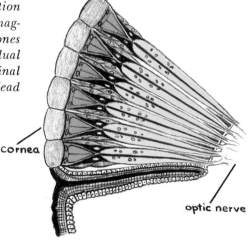

Transverse cut through a section of a dragonfly's eye, greatly magnified. The crystalline cones (shown in blue) of the individual ommatidia end in the retinal rods (shown in red), which lead into the optic nerve.

cornea

optic nerve

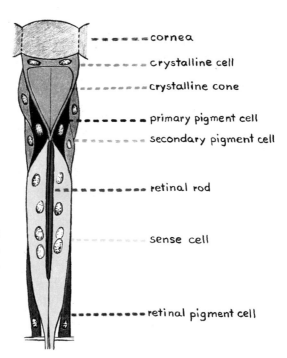

cornea

crystalline cell

crystalline cone

primary pigment cell

secondary pigment cell

retinal rod

sense cell

retinal pigment cell

A single ommatidium. The different portions are color-coded for easy identification.

rounded by a dark mantle, which absorbs all light rays except those that form a straight line with the axis of the cone.

As shown in the diagram, an insect's compound eye can distinguish individual visual impressions only to the extent that the image falls into the field of separate ommatidia. This means that an insect's vision increases with the number of ommatidia, much in the way a mosaic picture becomes more accurate if a greater number of stones is used to depict the object that it is supposed to reproduce. By and large, any insect's ability to distinguish shapes is poor in comparison with that of man, but this deficiency is made up by other advantages. Many insects have excellent color vision and are able to see ultraviolet light. Many can also distinguish polar-

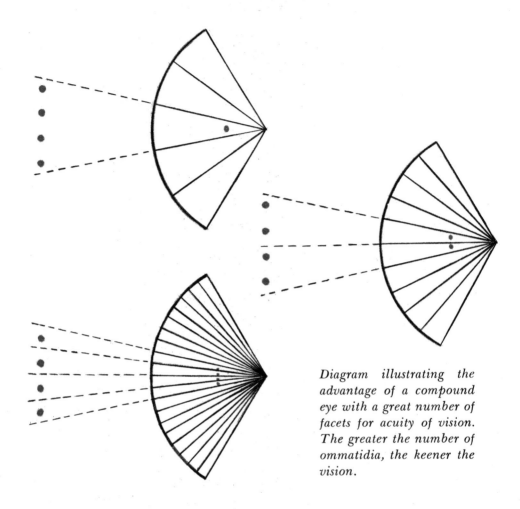

Diagram illustrating the advantage of a compound eye with a great number of facets for acuity of vision. The greater the number of ommatidia, the keener the vision.

ized from unpolarized light. Undoubtedly many other aspects of insects' vision are still unknown, and attaining certain knowledge of how insects view the world around them must inevitably remain an unfulfilled wish for human beings.

The large size of the typical dragonfly's eye is directly connected with the keenness of its vision. It may have more than three times the number of ommatidia found in a honeybee's eye. A maximum of 30,000 individual facets, which face in all directions, including backward and downward, gives these insects a range of vision that outstrips that of any other insect. Moreover, the head is hollowed out in the rear, and may be rotated freely on the slender neck, thus even further increasing the dragonfly's visual field. Some naturalists claim that dragonflies can perceive movement at a distance of as much as forty feet, which is most unusual for the insect's type of fixed-focus eye. Not even the slightest movement escapes those wonderful eyes, so that it is almost impossible to sneak up on a dragonfly sunning itself between meals. Anyone who doubts this should try it sometime.

Evidence that these insects rely mainly on vision rather than on the senses of touch and smell is found in the extremely small size of their antennae. This is unusual, for the antennae of most adult insects are quite prominent, and serve as indispensable aids for survival because of their combined function of nose and tactile organ. Finding food, locating and attracting mates, detecting enemies—all these vital activities would be impossible for many insects without their antennae.

In contrast, dragonflies hardly seemed to notice when experimenters removed their tiny, hairlike antennae. The individuals without antennae continued to live as normally as those that still had them and went about their daily activities without the slightest indication that they lacked a seemingly important sense organ.

The mouthparts of the Odonata, as well as their eyes, are well adapted to their way of life. The mandibles are extremely large and toothed. So is the lower lip, or labium, which is also hooked to enable the insect to grasp its prey firmly. The mandibles act as a scissors-like instrument with which the food is cut up into small pieces.

The thorax, the middle portion of its body, differs in important details from that of other insects. Broad and box-like, the thorax is slanted in a way that causes all the legs to be situated forward, close to the head, while the wings are located behind the hindmost pair of legs. Clustered beneath the mouth, the legs cannot be used for walking on the ground, although a dragonfly can cling to plants, rocks, and other convenient surfaces when it wants to rest. The inability to walk does not hamper this creature, most of

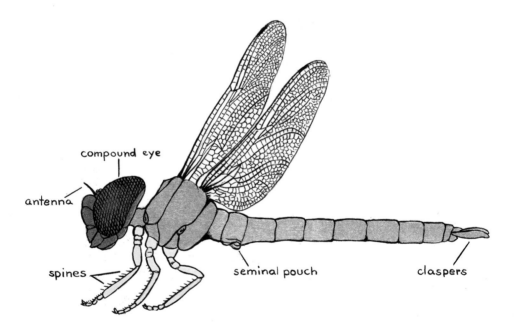

Diagram of a dragonfly, color-coded for easy identification.

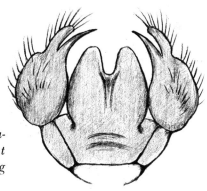

A dragonfly's lower lip, or labium, which forms an efficient tool for grasping and holding prey.

whose important activities are carried out on the wing, but the legs function as valuable aids in capturing prey. Their forward location enables the dragonfly to use them as a basket-like trap for the flying insects it hunts. Long, sharp spines on the legs securely pin down any captured fly or mosquito. The prey is then transferred to the mouth and quickly cut to pieces and devoured.

The dragonfly's most outstanding feature undoubtedly is its special flight structures. The two pairs of wings are large and broad, of almost equal length and width. A tight network of bracing veins gives the wing membrane great strength, and enables some of the large species of dragonflies to rank among the most powerful fliers in the insect world, despite the fact that their flight-muscle structure is considered primitive compared to that of such insects as flies and bees.

That the dragonfly is limited in its wing movements becomes evident even to a casual observer. It has no mechanism, for instance, for flexing its wings backward to make them lie flat over its back—an ability evolved even in the ancient cockroaches.

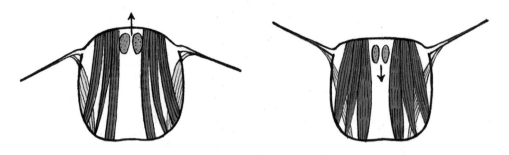

Flight muscles of an advanced insect.

The flight mechanism of dragonflies differs radically from that of more advanced insects. All higher insects such as flies and bees execute most wing movements by means of "indirect" flight muscles, attached not to the wings, but to a plate on the back between the wings. When these muscles contract, the plate is depressed, thereby lifting the wings. In addition, the flight muscles of advanced insects generate tremendous energy and have a rapid rhythm of contraction. As a result, a bee is able to beat its wings some 250 times per

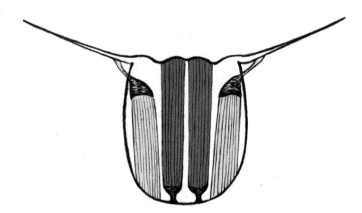

Diagram of the dragonfly's "primitive" flight muscles. The enormously developed direct flight muscles (shown in yellow), attached to the wings, play a more important part than the indirect flight muscles (shown in red).

second, and certain small flies are said to have a wingbeat of approximately 1000 times per second. Compare this to the 30 times per second which dragonflies can manage, and you will understand why their flight mechanism is considered primitive.

All Odonata move their wings with the aid of very strong and well-developed "direct" flight muscles, attached to the wing bases. The two pairs of wings move independently from each other, not being synchronized as are those of bees. The tendency to uneven, flickering flight caused by this arrangement is more or less compensated for by the stabilizing influence of the long, slender abdomen.

Because of their primitive flight mechanism, biologists consider these insects to be *paleopterous,* a word of Greek derivation meaning "ancient-winged," and representing a very early form. It is assumed today that all flight, in insects as well as in birds, most likely originated with an ability to glide. Dragonflies, with their long, slender bodies and their large, stiffly outspread wings, resemble glider planes, and, in fact, they served as models for early airplanes. One of the first French planes was named "Demoiselle" in honor of the dragonfly.

If all this talk about primitive flight structures sounds as though dragonflies cannot compete with the more advanced flying insects, we should keep in mind that it is the latter who are the victims of the "ancient-winged" predators, and not the other way around. All their complex, advanced body features do not protect the flies, midges, and mosquitoes from the strength, agility, and keen vision of the dragonfly survivors of a distant past.

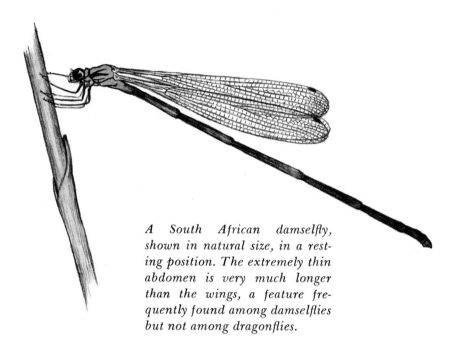

A South African damselfly, shown in natural size, in a resting position. The extremely thin abdomen is very much longer than the wings, a feature frequently found among damselflies but not among dragonflies.

The dragonfly's greatly elongated abdomen—third and last of an insect's main body divisions—also has some unique features not found in any other insect group. The male has both a special pouch on the second segment and a pair of claspers at the very tip. The function of these appendages will be discussed in the chapter that follows.

The shape of the abdomen varies with the species. In the majority, it resembles a slender rod, being not much thicker than a heavy needle in some damselflies. It is no wonder that many people believe this thin abdomen to be a stinger. Dragonflies cannot sting, of course, and are perfectly harmless to people—with the exception, of course, of the careless person who has managed to get hold of a large individual and has failed to keep his fingers out of the reach of those powerful jaws.

Many species of the subfamily *Libellulinae,* which includes the common North American ten-spotted dragonfly, are distinguished by a strongly depressed, flat, broad abdomen. These dragonflies thus appear stouter and more heavy-bodied than the rest of their relatives.

The color patterns of dragonflies, often concentrated on the abdomen, are believed to play an important part not only in the recognition between the sexes but also in the encounters between rival males trying to establish breeding territories. We shall learn more about this interesting part of the dragonfly's life in the next chapter, which deals with the search for a mate and the beginning of a new generation.

Mating Rituals

The most important and serious task in the relatively short life of the adult dragonfly—as in that of all other insects— is to seek a mate and propagate its kind. The first step toward that goal takes place when the male arrives at the breeding site and selects a territory, which is then vigorously defended against any encroachment by other males.

The type of breeding site as well as the size of the territory may vary considerably with the species. Generally, small damselflies establish limited territories close to the water surface and vegetation. The size of the territory tends to increase with the size of the male claiming it. Thus, a large, male green darner may patrol an entire pond and defend it against other males of the same species, while at the same time tolerating male damselflies who defend small territories at the edge of the same pond.

Territorial behavior also varies with the species. Among many damselflies, it appears to be not at all highly developed. The majority of dragonflies, on the other hand, stake out and defend a territory often days before the females arrive. Such behavior plays an important role not only in assuring that no one locality will be overcrowded, but also in forcing other males into availing themselves of all possible locations, which may include heretofore unexplored but highly suitable breeding places.

Defending a territory against other males rarely includes actual fighting. This follows the general pattern in the animal world, where fighting between rival males usually does not end with the death or serious injury of one of the combatants, and very often is a quickly decided, bloodless contest. This is especially fortunate in the case of the dragonflies, for actual combat would almost invariably end with the death of both males. Instead, the male defending the territory performs what biologists call a "threat display," which consists of dashing toward an intruding male, but without touching him. After engaging in this mock combat a number of times, the intruder usually leaves; if he does not, the two rivals may then begin a mild form of aerial jousting that hardly ever has a fatal ending. Generally, the weaker male soon turns to flee and is pursued for a short distance by the victor.

In many cases, the brilliant colors of male dragonflies seem to play a role in threat displays. It has been observed that some males raise their abdomens in order to show certain colors while rushing to meet an intruder. When one scientist altered the color of the abdomen in such individuals, they scored much more poorly in finding a mate because they were less successful in defending their territories.

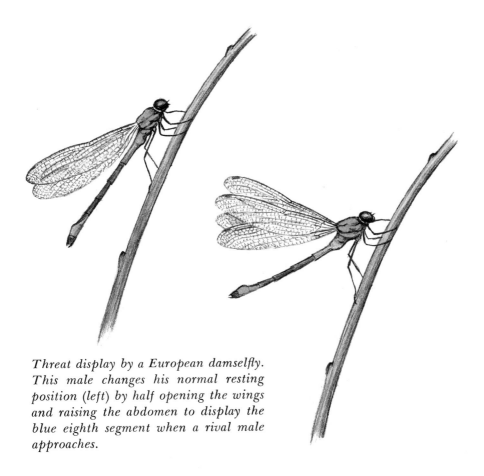

Threat display by a European damselfly. This male changes his normal resting position (left) by half opening the wings and raising the abdomen to display the blue eighth segment when a rival male approaches.

The individual color patterns displayed by the various species are of prime importance in the recognition between the sexes. This is to be expected from insects such as dragonflies, whose vision is so well developed, and is in contrast to most other insects, which locate and attract their mates through their senses of smell or hearing.

Experiments with male damselflies presented with artificial models of females have disclosed some of the features essential for recognition by the opposite sex. Most important seems to be the characteristic color pattern of the

An unreceptive female signals her unwillingness to mate by bending her abdomen downward, thus discouraging the male from pursuing her.

species, which must be present for the male to be attracted at all. In addition, the female model must have the typical form of the head, the thorax, and at least one wing—and that wing has to have the correct degree of translucence. The model also has to be moved back and forth a certain number of times per second before the male starts the courtship performance.

Although the experiments confirmed many of the assumptions about sex recognition advanced by biologists, some interesting new points were discovered. One is the fact that the degree of wing membrane translucence plays so important a part; the other is the apparent unimportance of the number of wings the model of the female may have. A model with five wings is not more acceptable than one with only a single wing of the proper size, shape, and translucence, which varies with each species, depending largely upon the pattern and density of the venation. The other wings may even be different in size and color without bothering the male in the least!

After the appropriate courtship, the details of which vary with the species, the male proceeds to mate with the female of his choice. Flying above her, he seizes her thorax with his legs. At this point, it quickly becomes evident whether or not the female is willing to accept her suitor. If she is unwilling, she flies on swiftly, thus evading his grip. Usually she is receptive, and slows down. The male immediately forms a loop of his abdomen and, with the aid of the two claspers at its very tip, firmly grasps the neck of the female. In many species, the female dragonfly has grooves at the back of her head into which the male's claspers fit perfectly.

As soon as the male has established a firm hold, he lets go of the female's thorax with his legs. Straightening his abdomen, he flies on in tandem with her below. Before executing this maneuver, however, he has transferred sperm from the genital opening at the tip of his abdomen to a special pouch located on the underside of the second ab-

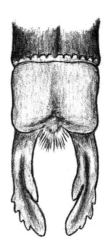

The claspers of a male damselfly, used to hold the female by the neck during mating.

A pair of European dragonflies in the wheel position, the culmination of the mating ritual.

dominal segment. This is a unique feature found in no other insect, and biologists still cannot agree on the reason for this anatomical oddity, or on the possible ways the unusual arrangement for transferring sperm from male to female might have evolved. For at this point the female must take action: forming a loop with her abdomen, she touches its tip to the male's sperm pouch, thus fertilizing her eggs. The two dragonflies now are in the so-called wheel position with the female upside down beneath the male, who still holds her firmly by the head. The wheel position is almost never assumed during flight; usually the male alights upon a stem or reed, to which he clings.

In the majority of insects, the comparatively brief act of mating terminates male-female association. They immediately part company to go about their own ways, the male to resume his normal way of life for whatever period of time is left to him, the female to assume all responsibility for depositing the eggs in such a way that the new generation gets the best possible chance of survival. Given the infinite variety of insect life, there are many exceptions to this general rule. The termite "king," for example, although he mates with the queen only once in his lifetime, remains with and attends her to the end of his life. At the other extreme, the male praying mantis must step lively after the nuptials to avoid becoming the larger female's wedding breakfast.

The behavior of dragonflies after their mating is quite remarkable, differing markedly from that of most other insects. Not only does the male usually remain with the female for quite some time, but he may actually escort her to sites well suited for depositing her eggs.

The male of many dragonfly species continues to hold the female, again flying in tandem with her until they have reached a suitable location, often in the same territory he initially defended.

A good example of male participation in the task of egg-laying is found in the ruby-spot damselfly, a common species of both temperate and tropical America. The female deposits her eggs in the stems of aquatic plants. After a pair of ruby-spots have located a suitable plant, the male usually

*The complete courtship, mating, and egg-laying ritual. At left:
Male pursues female, while she slows down; male then grasps female
around the neck with his claspers; straightening out his abdomen,
male flies ahead with female below in tandem. Below: Couple in
wheel position, with female fertilizing her eggs from the male's
genital pouch. Finally, eggs are laid in the water while the female
is still being held by the male.*

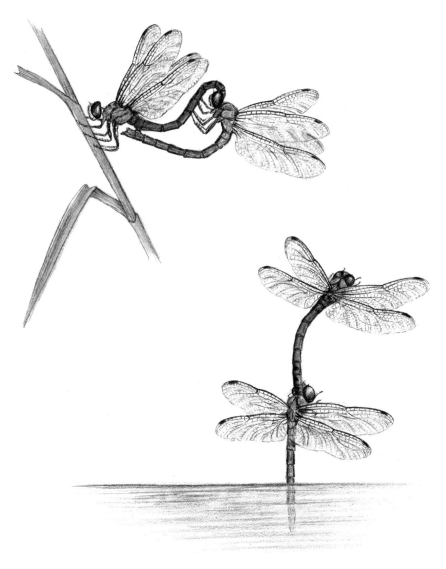

releases her and then sits, waiting, while she backs into the water to insert her eggs into the plant stems below the surface. Sometimes, however, he may continue to hold her during the entire process of egg-laying. Only when the mission is completed do the two damselflies part company.

An even more fascinating spectacle is presented by damselflies of a European species whose females lay their eggs directly in the water. A pair of these damselflies, which appear only in late summer, engage in a graceful aerial ballet with light and elegant movements that belie the fact that the two performers are involved in the serious task of propagating the species. Flying in tandem, they flit over the surface of the pond in a rhythmic up-and-down movement. Every time they approach the water, the abdomen of the female swings downward to deposit another egg.

Unattended female dragonfly depositing her eggs in the sand on the bottom of a brook.

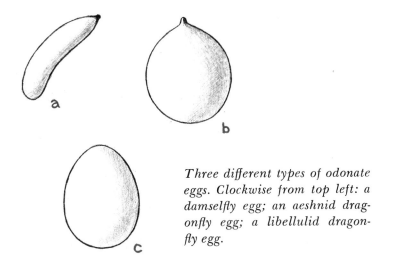

Three different types of odonate eggs. Clockwise from top left: a damselfly egg; an aeshnid dragonfly egg; a libellulid dragonfly egg.

In certain dragonfly species the male releases the female after mating and then guides her to a good breeding site, hovering above while she lays her eggs and driving away any male intruder who may happen along.

Not all male dragonflies display such solicitous behavior: in some species female dragonflies have to accomplish the task of selecting a site and depositing the eggs without any male guidance. The breeding locations all have one thing

Stem of an aquatic plant with a section removed to show the inserted damselfly eggs. Some damselflies insert their eggs into the submerged leaves of aquatic plants.

in common: they are below the surface of the water. In other respects the sites differ considerably. One species breeds in lagoons where the water is brackish, another selects the base of a waterfall, despite the churning, rushing torrent typical of that part of the stream.

Depending upon the species, eggs may be laid in a stem or a leaf of an aquatic plant, which the female slits with the tip of her abdomen to insert the eggs, or in piles of mud or decaying plant material. Some females simply drop the eggs over the water in flight. These eggs are surrounded with a jelly-like mass and quickly sink to the bottom of the pond or become attached to plants as they sink. One large,

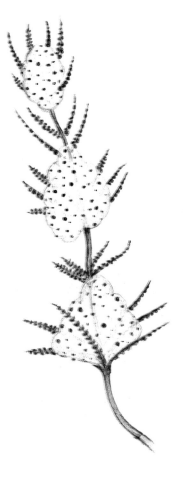

An aquatic plant with dragonfly eggs attached to the leaves by a jelly-like coating in which they are embedded.

black and yellow European dragonfly is found along the brooks of meadows, woods, and forests. When the time for egg-laying comes, the female follows the brook up through the woods until she comes to the clear, cool waters not far from the spring that feeds the brook. Suddenly, the female begins to dip her abdomen through the shallow water and into the fine sand at the bottom. Again and again she rises and dips down to plant an egg in the sand each time, for she knows instinctively that her larvae need cool, running water for their development.

Whatever the special nature of the breeding site selected by dragonfly parents, it is in all cases designed to offer the maximum chance for survival to the tiny larvae which eventually hatch from the eggs.

Underwater Sojourn

The eggs laid by the female dragonfly or damselfly may hatch in a few days, or incubation may be as long as nine months. The length of the period between the depositing of an egg and the hatching of the larva depends on the species as well as on the season. Unseasonably cool weather may delay the development.

When the tiny hatchlings finally emerge from the eggs, they find themselves in an underwater world filled with a host of enemies. Other aquatic insects and small fish consider them fair prey, and their ranks are soon decimated by the predations of these larger creatures. However, some of the dragonfly offspring survive and grow, and soon become formidable predators themselves.

The odonate larva is a peculiar-looking creature. Because these insects have what is known as a gradual development—which differs from both the direct and the complex type—their larvae are commonly called nymphs, and sometimes naiads. In ancient Greek mythology, naiads were beautiful

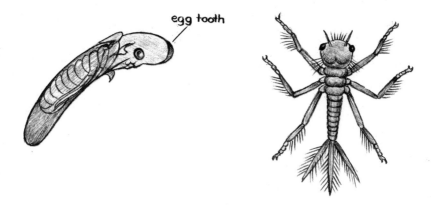

egg tooth

A hatching damselfly egg and the new hatchling. The hairs on the legs and gills usually disappear in later stages of larval development.

maidens inhabiting lakes and streams. There could hardly be a less appropriate name for the dragonfly nymph, for it looks like an ugly little monster. All the same, it is a remarkable creature with a number of unusual anatomical features that help it to hold its own in an underwater world where sudden death lurks everywhere.

As mentioned earlier, dragonfly nymphs have a superficial resemblance to overgrown earwigs. Their coloring, usually brown or greenish, is adapted to blend well with the aquatic vegetation, mud, sand, silt, and decaying plant material that forms their habitat. Often solid-colored but sometimes mottled or banded with rather somber hues, some nymphs possess the ability, to a limited degree, of changing their color to adapt it to darker or lighter backgrounds as they move from one place to another.

Because of their aquatic existence at the bottom of ponds and streams, the nymphs need a special breathing mechanism capable of extracting oxygen from the water. Such a mechanism is provided in the gills, with which odonate larvae are equipped. These gills differ from those found in higher animals—fish, for example—in that they are filled with tiny air tubes called trachea, which carry oxygen directly to the cells. All insects except some very primitive kinds breathe by means of a complex system of trachea which, in terrestrial insects, have external openings called spiracles, situated along the sides of the thorax and abdomen.

The gills of damselfly nymphs are visible as three finlike appendages located at the tip of the abdomen. This, together with their smaller eyes and longer antennae, distinguishes them from their more robust dragonfly cousins, whose gills are not externally visible. The internal gills of the dragonfly nymph are one of its most remarkable features, because in addition to serving as a respiratory system, they also act as a propeller that enables the larva to move quickly when conditions require it.

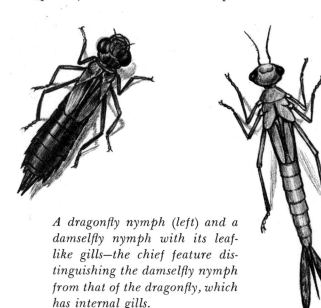

A dragonfly nymph (left) and a damselfly nymph with its leaflike gills—the chief feature distinguishing the damselfly nymph from that of the dragonfly, which has internal gills.

*Transverse cut through the ab-
domen of a dragonfly nymph.
The gills (shown in red) supply
the insect with oxygen.*

The small, flat gills of the dragonfly larva are arranged in rows along the sides of the posterior part of its intestine, which is enlarged and very muscular. In order to breathe, the nymph sucks fresh water through the anal opening by expanding and contracting its intestinal chamber. After the oxygen has been extracted, the water is expelled. If the nymph is disturbed in any way, it can contract the chamber so suddenly that the water is expelled in a jet of such force that the insect is propelled forward with considerable speed. It has been reported that the larva of the green darner dragonfly is able to move at a speed of about twenty inches per second.

Responses by the larva to possible danger are extremely quick: small hairs at the tail end act as very sensitive tactile organs. The slightest stimulation of these hairs causes the intestinal chamber to contract immediately, resulting in the nymph being propelled violently through the water, often out of the reach of a hungry predator. The nymph's mechanism is actually the prototype of jet propulsion—a principle employed successfully in nature millions of years before man appeared on this planet.

Because of their external gills, damselfly larvae do not
have this convenient escape device. Being also smaller and
more delicate, they tend to hide in the aquatic vegetation,
waiting to pounce upon prey that passes by, rather than to
hunt actively for it.

The apparatus by which odonate nymphs capture their
prey is an extraordinary device not found anywhere else
in the insect world. The lower lip, or labium, of the larva
is enormously lengthened. Hinge joints at the base and the
middle permit the lip to be pulled back and folded beneath
the head when not in use. One entomologist has compared
the labium to the snout of a gas mask, since in the resting

Seen from below; closed.

Seen from the side; closed.

*Seen from below and the
side; partly extended.*

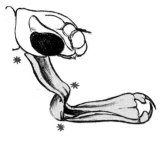

*Seen from the side, fully
extended.*

*Capture-mask of a dragonfly nymph in several positions. Hinge
joints are marked by red asterisks in lower-right illustration.*

position it forms a mask that covers part of the nymph's face. As soon as the insect spies an unsuspecting prey within the reach of the extended mask, the labium is shot forward with lightning speed to grab the victim. The front part of the mask ends in two hooked lobes which firmly hold the

A dragonfly nymph with a captured mosquito larva.

prey, while it is drawn back within reach of the strong, sharp mandibles. When cutting up and chewing its food, the nymph uses the labium as a sort of plate to catch any morsel that may fall from the jaws.

For its size, the dragonfly larva is one of the most rapacious creatures known. It will tackle anything it can overwhelm, including animals larger than itself. Some of the big dragonfly nymphs occasionally become a nuisance when they establish themselves in fish hatcheries and prey upon the small fry. With this exception, dragonfly nymphs, like the adults, are highly beneficial insects, because the bulk of their diet consists of such pests as mosquito larvae, and they are hearty eaters. Anyone who has ever attempted to raise nymphs in an aquarium soon finds out that they require an almost incredible amount of food. Keeping them supplied with a sufficient number of mosquito larvae can be a formidable job because they have to be fed at least every other day in order to keep them alive and healthy. One of the great authorities on dragonflies, Philip C. Calvert, once wrote an article on raising dragonfly nymphs, based on his own experiences. A single nymph which he kept in an aquarium, and which took almost one year to complete its larval development, consumed more than 3000 mosquito larvae—about ten a day—plus a few hundred other aquatic insects during that period. Multiply this by the number of nymphs found in ponds, lakes, and pools, and you will get an idea of how many obnoxious and potentially dangerous mosquitoes are eliminated as larvae by the immature dragonflies. If this is combined with the great number of adult mosquitoes captured by the mature dragonflies, it is easy to see why these insects should be protected wherever they appear, if not only because they are beautiful.

The nymph's success in capturing prey depends to a large extent on its ability to locate it. Here, as with the adults, keen vision plays an important part, at least in the larger species. The nymphs of smaller dragonflies, as well as those of damselflies, seem to rely on their antennae, which are fairly long, and on other tactile organs rather than on their relatively small eyes, to detect prey in the water around them. The larger species, however, all have big eyes with excellent vision, as experiments have proved. The eyes of these nymphs are so placed on the head that the insect enjoys very good binocular vision, enabling the nymph to estimate correctly the size of the prey and the distance at which it is located. As soon as the waiting larva spots a likely victim, it turns to face it. The eyes are positioned in

Mosquito larvae and pupae, the favorite food of dragonfly nymphs. In contrast to the pupal stages of most other insects, mosquito pupae are active and move around in the water.

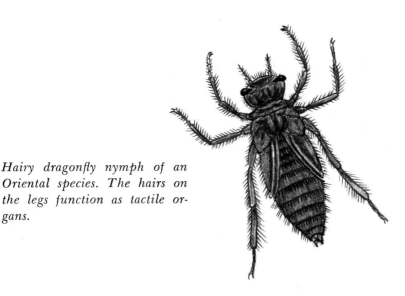

Hairy dragonfly nymph of an Oriental species. The hairs on the legs function as tactile organs.

a way that permits a group of the inner ommatidia to act as a "range finder," because their optical axes intersect at the exact point within the reach of the capture-mask's hooks when it is fully extended. As soon as the prey moves into the area of this intersection, the mask is shot forward to seize the prey.

The speed with which the lower lip moves is almost beyond belief. It is much too fast for the human eye to follow: tests by scientists have shown that the forward movement requires only three hundredths of a second. Twice this time is needed for retraction, so that the entire act of grasping and pulling a victim back within reach of the jaws takes less than one tenth of a second.

The question of how the nymphs manage to achieve this incredible speed has intrigued scientists, who do not yet fully understand what causes the lower lip to be shot forward in this manner. It is assumed, however, that a contraction of certain muscles forces the blood to rush to the head, thus triggering the forward movement. Further study will undoubtedly provide a more complete answer of how the mechanism works.

The importance of vision for all large-eyed dragonfly nymphs in capturing their prey was proved by tests which kept these insects in total darkness in an aquarium liberally stocked with other aquatic insects. Not even over a period of days were the nymphs able to catch any of the other insects. They would have starved if the period of artificial darkness had been prolonged. Among other things, this experiment showed that such dragonfly larvae are not active by night but hunt during daytime only.

In order to prove conclusively that the large-eyed dragonfly nymphs use only their vision to locate their prey, one zoologist covered the eyes of several captives with black paint. Thus incapacitated, the nymphs were unable to feed themselves, catching not a single insect over a period of days. The most interesting situation, however, arose when the larvae had only one eye covered with black paint. At first, all these one-eyed nymphs were unable to capture anything because their binocular vision had been destroyed along with the "range finder" which ordinarily enables them to pinpoint their prey's location. As a result, the one-eyed larvae always struck to either the right or the left of any insect they tried to capture. Many of these artificially incapacitated nymphs could not adapt to their disability and starved in the midst of plenty. A few, however, were not so easily discouraged and, after many unsuccessful attempts, finally learned to use their one good eye in a way that enabled them to catch at least enough prey to survive.

They managed this by creeping up sideways, in a crablike fashion, to a prospective victim. Then, as they shot the mask forward, they made a part turn so that they faced their prey. This maneuver proved successful often enough to keep these resourceful nymphs provided with food.

Undoubtedly, this particular test proved that even a single compound eye of the type found in dragonfly larvae is capable of some crude kind of binocular vision. The most remarkable fact to emerge from the test is the difference, among individuals of the same species, in the capacity to learn and to successfully overcome handicaps. Such observations should help to counteract the widespread tendency to assume that the behavior and actions of a single individual of any given species, especially among lower animals, is a blueprint of the behavior of all the individuals within that group. Anyone who takes the time and effort to observe dragonfly nymphs in captivity will find that they offer excellent proof of a wide range of differences among individuals of the same species. At first they all are very shy and tend to hide or even play dead. Some, however, will become quite tame, and after a few weeks, may even become bold enough to accept food offered at the end of a thin stick. This ability to learn and to adapt to unusual situations may have contributed to the success of dragonflies in holding their own in a world of constant changes that have proven fatal to many other animal groups.

As the odonate nymph grows, it periodically sheds its outer skin. The process of replacing the tight, old skin with a new, roomier one is called molting. This is the only way any immature insect can grow. The adult insect no longer molts, and remains the same size as long as it lives. Most insects with gradual development molt about five times during their larval development. Dragonfly nymphs molt anywhere from ten to fifteen times, and frequently change their color along with their skin, especially in the early stages.

After completing the larval growth, the time for the final molt arrives. This always occurs during summer

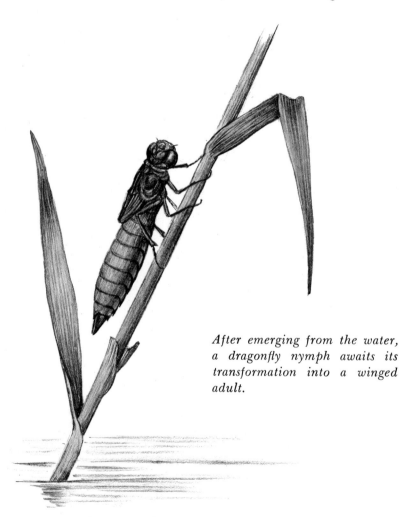

After emerging from the water, a dragonfly nymph awaits its transformation into a winged adult.

months, usually between May and August. When the time comes, the nymph suddenly loses all interest in its aquatic environment, and leaves the water for the first time since it hatched from the egg, months or even years before. Slowly, awkwardly, the future dragonfly crawls up on the stem of a reed, a jutting rock, or a riverbank, and then sits quietly waiting.

The cycle is about to be completed: very soon, within a matter of hours, the miracle of transformation will once again repeat itself, and a glittering, winged dragonfly will leave its drab nymphal shell and take off for a life in the air and the sun.

A Picture Gallery of
Dragonfly Beauties

In the insect class, the two orders most noted for the beauty of many of their members are the Lepidoptera, which include butterflies and moths, and the Coleoptera, the beetles. Almost everyone knows examples of these groups, which are often reproduced in ornaments and jewelry.

Much less familiar are the attractive species of other orders. Even dragonflies, which have a greater percentage of beautifully colored members than any insect order except the two named above, are relatively little known to the average person. This can be attributed perhaps partly to

A common European dragonfly. Only the male has a bright blue abdomen.

the fact that dragonflies, because of their swift flight and specialized way of life, are not as easy to observe as are flower-visiting butterflies. In addition, those species with the most beautiful coloration lose their colors shortly after death, and become drab and rather sorry-looking things. In contrast to butterflies and beetles, which with rare exceptions are remarkably colorfast, there is no way of displaying mounted specimens of dragonflies in museums or other collections to show the beauty of their coloring to people unable to see them alive in their own habitat.

The reasons for the loss of color after the dragonfly's death are based upon the fact that the most beautiful hues

A handsome European dragonfly.

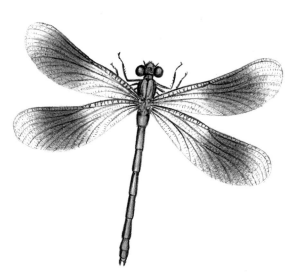

Male of a European broad-winged damselfly.

are not the result of coloring matter. As mentioned earlier in the book, all the metallic, pure colors of the dragonflies are created by submicroscopic tissue structures which selectively absorb and reflect light waves. The same principle applies to such colors in butterflies, beetles, and certain other insects. When structural colors occur in tissues that are stable, the structural colors are also stable, and remain colorfast almost indefinitely after the death of the animal. Stable tissues are those fully formed and already "dead" in the live animal—such as the scales on the wings of butterflies— and therefore not subject to any further change. But when the colors are found in tissues that change even slightly after death, the incredibly delicate arrangement that makes

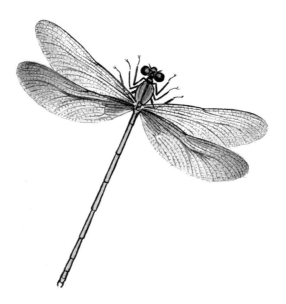

An Oriental damselfly. The multicolored wings gleam in pure iridescent hues.

South African beauty of the libellulid family.

Fully mature male of a familiar
European species.

Male of a handsome European damsel-fly, relative of the American black-winged damselfly.

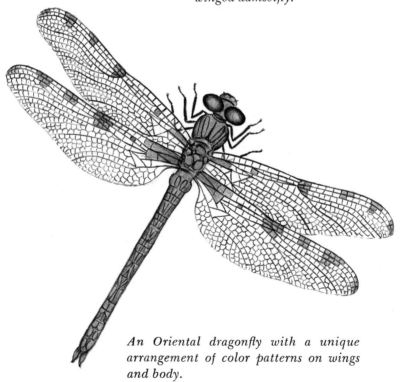

An Oriental dragonfly with a unique arrangement of color patterns on wings and body.

Another Oriental damselfly beauty. This type of wing coloration is relatively rare among the Odonata.

possible the reflection of certain light waves is eliminated, and with it the colors. Pigment colors, which are independent of the structure of the tissue that contains them, are not subject to this kind of fading.

Because the body tissues of dragonflies shrink as they dry after death, the jewel-like colors of the eyes and body disappear astonishingly, leaving a dull-looking insect without a trace of its former radiance.

Hence, the beauty of the most attractive species can be preserved only in color pictures of the live insects—and even

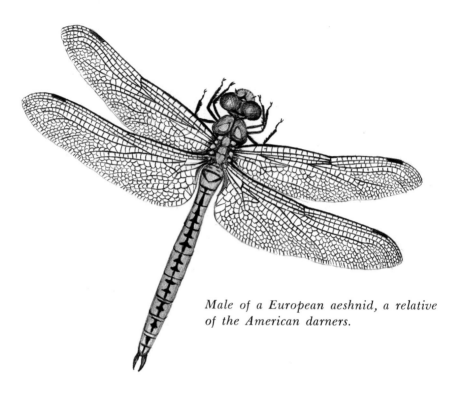

Male of a European aeshnid, a relative of the American darners.

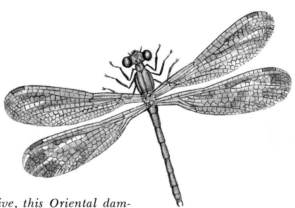

Small but attractive, this Oriental damselfly can hold its own in comparison with any larger species.

then only partially. The trouble with such pictures is that the gleaming, shifting structural colors, because of their very nature, are impossible to duplicate precisely with the pigments we have to use for such reproductions.

All the same, illustrations do convey some idea of the splendor of the living dragonfly. In this final chapter is a selection of elegant species from around the globe. Each one is testimony for the claim that dragonflies should be protected as much for their beauty as for their role as useful predators in the control of mosquitoes and other insect pests.

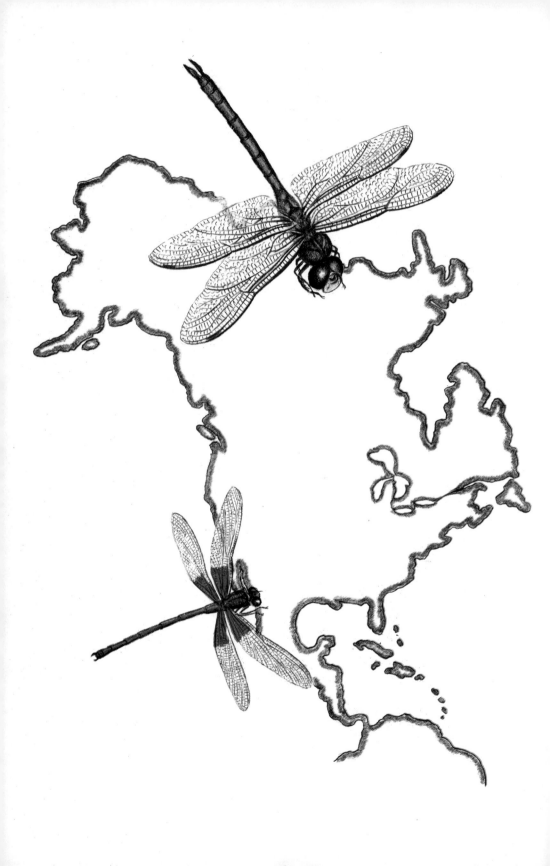

A Guide to
North American Dragonflies

Roughly 10 per cent—some 420 species—of the total number of the world's Odonata occur on the North American continent. Many of these species are comparatively rare and are not often seen by the average observer, especially those that are restricted to a specific habitat, such as a swamp, from which they never stray very far. Quite a few species are common in many parts of the continent, and some travel considerable distances from the water in which their larval development took place and to which they return to launch a new generation. The majority of the most familiar species belong to five large groups: the narrow-winged damselflies, the broad-winged damselflies, the aeshnids, libellulids, and gomphids. In the pages that follow we shall see representatives of all these families, as well as a member of the spread-winged damselflies. In order to make identification easier, all the illustrations are life-sized. Identification in the field,

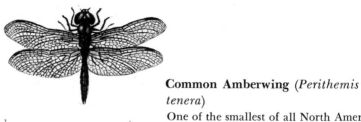

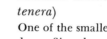

Common Amberwing (*Perithemis tenera*)

One of the smallest of all North American dragonflies, the amberwing belongs to the family Libellulidae. It is chiefly seen around swamps and ponds and usually does not range very far from the water, in contrast to many others of its group. In identifying this small species, the yellowish color of the wings is a good aid.

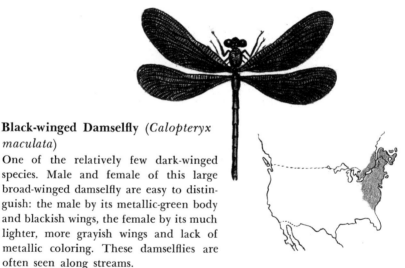

Black-winged Damselfly (*Calopteryx maculata*)

One of the relatively few dark-winged species. Male and female of this large broad-winged damselfly are easy to distinguish: the male by its metallic-green body and blackish wings, the female by its much lighter, more grayish wings and lack of metallic coloring. These damselflies are often seen along streams.

in contrast to that of collected specimens, must rely chiefly on features recognizable from a distance, such as size, coloring, wing spots or bands, and resting position.

84

The approximate range of each species is indicated on the small map that accompanies each illustration. Generally, damselflies are encountered more often in the immediate proximity of water, especially of ponds and swamps, near which some of the smaller dragonflies are also habitually seen.

Civil Bluet (*Enallagma civile*)
A small, slender, bright blue species belonging to the group known as narrow-winged damselflies. The wings of this family, which includes most North American damselfly species, are constricted at the base to form stalks. The civil bluet as well as a number of close relatives are found throughout North America and are often abundant around ponds and swamps. The female is somewhat paler.

Clubtail (*Gomphus vastus*)
A representative of the large dragonfly family Gomphidae. Members of this group are distinguished by compound eyes that are separated in the center, instead of meeting in a seam. In some species the segments are swollen to form the "club" that gives them their distinctive appearance. Clubtails are found mainly along streams and lakes.

85

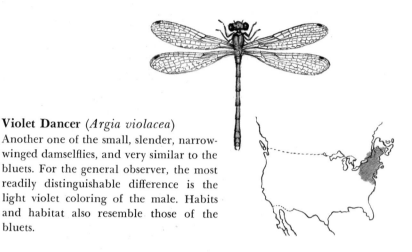

Violet Dancer (*Argia violacea*)
Another one of the small, slender, narrow-winged damselflies, and very similar to the bluets. For the general observer, the most readily distinguishable difference is the light violet coloring of the male. Habits and habitat also resemble those of the bluets.

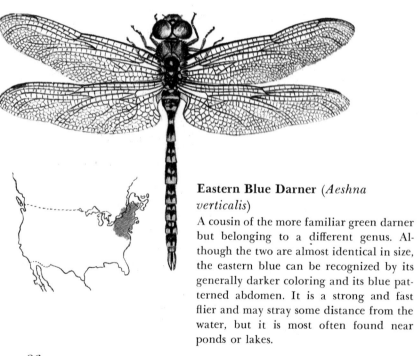

Eastern Blue Darner (*Aeshna verticalis*)
A cousin of the more familiar green darner but belonging to a different genus. Although the two are almost identical in size, the eastern blue can be recognized by its generally darker coloring and its blue patterned abdomen. It is a strong and fast flier and may stray some distance from the water, but it is most often found near ponds or lakes.

86

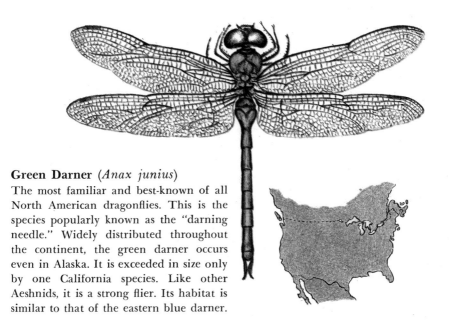

Green Darner (*Anax junius*)

The most familiar and best-known of all North American dragonflies. This is the species popularly known as the "darning needle." Widely distributed throughout the continent, the green darner occurs even in Alaska. It is exceeded in size only by one California species. Like other Aeshnids, it is a strong flier. Its habitat is similar to that of the eastern blue darner.

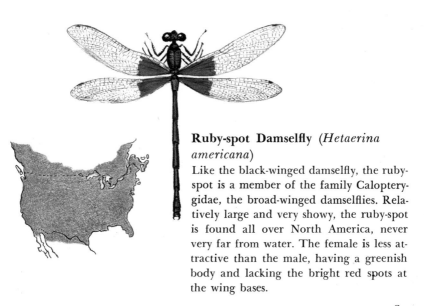

Ruby-spot Damselfly (*Hetaerina americana*)

Like the black-winged damselfly, the ruby-spot is a member of the family Calopterygidae, the broad-winged damselflies. Relatively large and very showy, the ruby-spot is found all over North America, never very far from water. The female is less attractive than the male, having a greenish body and lacking the bright red spots at the wing bases.

Elisa Skimmer (*Celithemis elisa*)
A large family, the common skimmers, or Libellulidae, include some of the most familiar species. Many members are distinguished by spotted or banded wings. Although some may have bright colors, they never display the metallic iridescent hues typical of so many Odonata. Skimmers are good fliers and often range far from water.

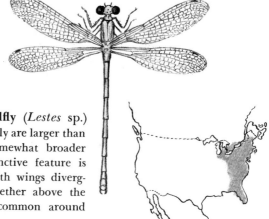

Spread-winged Damselfly (*Lestes* sp.)
The members of this family are larger than the bluets and have somewhat broader wings. Their most distinctive feature is their habit of resting with wings diverging, instead of held together above the body. They are quite common around ponds and swamps.

88

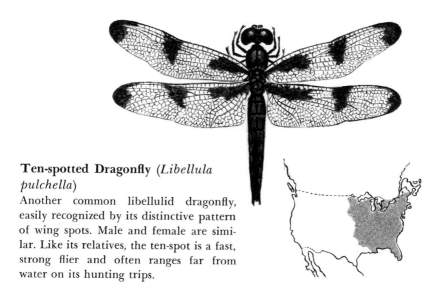

Ten-spotted Dragonfly (*Libellula pulchella*)

Another common libellulid dragonfly, easily recognized by its distinctive pattern of wing spots. Male and female are similar. Like its relatives, the ten-spot is a fast, strong flier and often ranges far from water on its hunting trips.

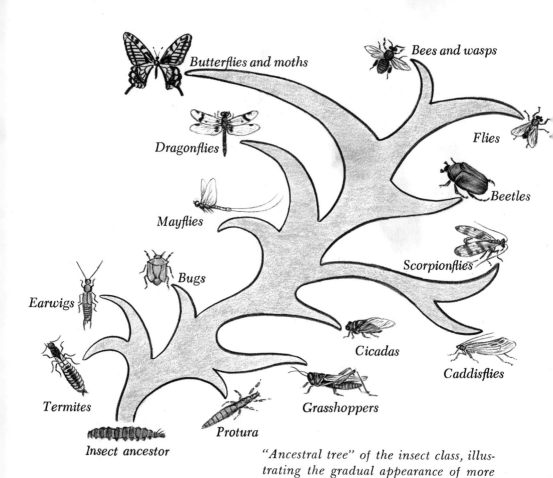

Butterflies and moths

Bees and wasps

Dragonflies

Flies

Mayflies

Beetles

Bugs

Scorpionflies

Earwigs

Termites

Cicadas

Caddisflies

Protura

Grasshoppers

Insect ancestor

"Ancestral tree" of the insect class, illustrating the gradual appearance of more advanced groups.

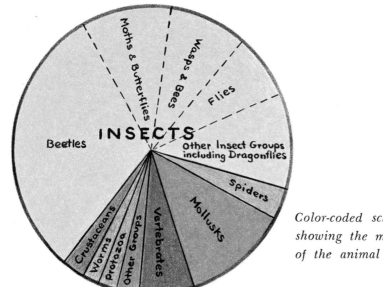

Moths & Butterflies

Wasps & Bees

Flies

Beetles

INSECTS

Other Insect Groups
including Dragonflies

Spiders

Crustaceans

Worms

Protozoa

Other Groups

Vertebrates

Mollusks

Color-coded schematic circle showing the major divisions of the animal kingdom.

Direct Development (Silverfish)

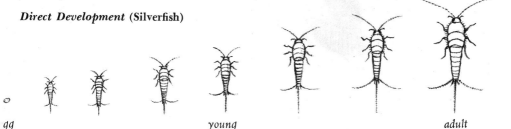

o

gg · *young* · *adult*

Gradual Development (Bug)

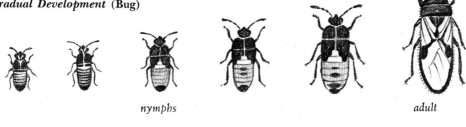

gg · *nymphs* · *adult*

Complex Development (Butterfly)

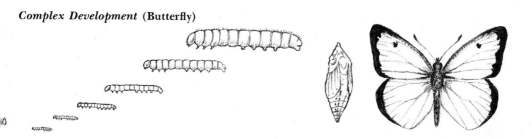

o

gg · *larvae* · *pupa* · *adult*

The three types of insect development. Insects such as drag-onflies go through a considerable transformation, but the absence of a pupal stage still puts them in the category of gradual, or incomplete, metamorphosis.

Index

Page numbers in italics refer to illustrations.